What Holds Us Here

What Holds Us Here

by

Betsy Warland

BuschekBooks

Canadian Cataloguing in Publication Data

Warland, Betsy, 1946-
    What holds us here

Poems.
ISBN 0-9699904-4-8

    I. Title.

PS8595.A7745W43 1998   C811'.54   C98-900264-0
PR9199.3.W37W43 1998

Other books by Betsy Warland:

Two Women in a Birth (Daphne Marlatt, co-author) (1994)
The Bat Had Blue Eyes (1993)
Proper Deafinitions (1990)
Double Negative (Daphne Marlatt, co-author) (1988)
serpent (w)rite (1987)
open is broken (1984)
A Gathering Instinct (1981)

Anthologies edited

Inversions: Writing by Dykes, Queers and Lesbians (1991)
Telling It: Women and Language Across Cultures (co-edited) (1990)
(f.)Lip — a newsletter of feminist innovative writing (co-editor) (1986-1989)
in the feminine: Women and Words/les femmes et les mots (1985)

What Holds Us Here
Printed and bound in Canada by Hignell Printing Limited, Winnipeg, Manitoba

Design: Marie Tappin

BuschekBooks
P.O.Box 74053
35 Beechwood Avenue
Ottawa, Ontario, K1M 2H9
Canada

Email: buschek.books@sympatico.ca
Website:
http://www3.sympatico.ca/buschek.books/home.html

John Buschek, editor

BuschekBooks
acknowledges the support of
the Canada Council for the Arts
for its publications

THE CANADA COUNCIL | LE CONSEIL DES ARTS
FOR THE ARTS | DU CANADA
SINCE 1957 | DEPUIS 1957

for Susan

Contents

Sight Unseen

In a Word

Shades of Meaning

Sight Unseen

Potato-Eaters

life classes

family

eating potatoes in

half-light

hands

like roots, faces

like their crop

still life

parents'   silence

on either side   of the

two in-between, their

uneasy effort

imploring the

lowered lids of their future

in the foreground

a small figure stands —

shape inserted

for compositional balance?

her back reveals nothing

she seems a shadow

on the table

five cups

(she must exist)

the only light

above her head

*

call from the backdoor each night

"come & get it!"

washing of hands

saying of Grace

each had their plate

(palette of orange, azure, robin's-egg blue, yellow, white)

their place

(palatableness of deceptions)

*

potatoes

she was sent daily for

unlit cellar

gleaming tendril-roots smooth as worms

quick twist

of kitchen knife

Bedroom at Arles

my small Amsterdam room

single bed, table, window, chair,

some images on the wall

a mirror

                              (a window a mirror)

then hopeful

his had two chairs, bed-pillows

sky walls

          sun-yellow bed

white companions me

                              (window mirror)

pencil pressed to paper

the opening of a book

      in solitude

              words rise like hungry trout

though it's

       the conversation of eyes we

ache for

               *

his blanket red upon his bed

to see so vividly &

               not be seen

eventually he stops signing his work, then

himself

             window mirror

           (   )

no one there

Dr. Gachet's Garden

red wall

gash wounding the horizon

erratic green & blue inside

/orderly outside

absence of human figures

though

built with them

in mind

*

the keeping

in &

out

the making of our meaning

Wheatfield with Lark

illuminated green in early summer innocent light

fragrant wind

wheat sway

to lie down

wanting only cirrus sky, exquisite

descant of lark

in-between the lean of green

the scarlet poppies, the

*

stubble foreground

barefeet knew

its sharp reality

first cutting

redwings' eggs

                    shattered on the ground

helplessness of

                    their cries

                    my hands

*

what was it about Paris?

the bulbs

the monochromatic bulbs

1884, 1885, 1886

     waiting

for the

right light

      colour shooting skyward unfold/exploding in the very act of

Portrait of the Artist

his eyes

        following

in

Musee D'Orsay

not the eyes'

        invitation

of Ingre's

"la Grand Odalisque"

nor the eyes'

        repleteness

of Da Vinci's

"Mona Lisa"

but his eyes'

        assessing

hard-edged

glare

*

translucent green & blue

swirl around

    like water like air

        (his face an open wound)

    flame of his hair

        (going up in anger)

  him or

      someone else

you would cross the street

know he was right

Fields Under Stormy Sky

what is

I

but a broken line?

*

far away the fields now far away

green of

lark with no lark

turbulent azure grey

trace of white giving way

24

*

distance of despair

comforting at the edge of a highrise roof

jumping

more to fly than die

(away-away)

yet we fall

we fall

the details rushing to meet us

*

his skies

could not

hold him.

Stuffed Kalong

he had his bat too

though not out of the blue

his was stuffed, stretched like a prehistoric crucifix

                                        The Father

the father

                    dark background against wings' orange light

Icarus, the sun

                        we fall

                                    we fall

                        Our Father Not

in heaven though

his will was done

half bird, half mouse

                    certainty his salvation

Portrait of the Artist

to not be seen

know the intent

smell the fear of the

turned back

with effacement

not to lose face when

                only your own eyes meet you

not to lose sight

      how

brush, pen

embrace you

*

when he left Nuenen

his self-portraits began

                                        (who is you?)

how to keep track of

first, once a year,

then frequently upon

moving to Paris

                        windows thrown open

more at home

yet not

the you so here

still there

            still   there

        eye of the storm

*

last look

he paints his death mask

cadaver complexion

cadere,

to fall

fall

*

after...

how face forgets

pain, abandons lines

to understand this,

desire it, yet

fear the loss

*

all lines require

years of effort

Portrait of Dr. Gachet

he leans on the table

with the posture of one who listens

we do not see the speaker,

only through his eyes:

is this a conversation?

where are the words?

                        words...

we miss them desperately

yet wonder what they allay

argument (Gaugin leaves) he cuts off

part of his ear
                        (ear the open-wound of hearing

the eyes of Dr. Gachet

kind yet weary — he's seen it all

what is there between them?

                                        a table, red

Wheatfield with Crows

quake of emotions

inmotion, impossible to stand up

stand it

unlike Frost's roads

his seemed no different

sometimes two roads are

still one

how an isolate talks to

himself as if someone's there —

pauses, listens —

                    laughs at the jokes

how blocked energy

turns in on

itself

poppies, buck-

shot of crows cawing beauty

there was more than one hand on the gun, Vincent,

i will say it now though each

would deny it

Boats on the Beach

colour   memory

memory   colour

the simple happiness

of those four boats

no human figures, no destinations,

just their boatness

while four, off-shore recede

into a wave into a cloud

foreground, centre,

   a yellow box

washed up on shore

                                   robin's-egg-sky arching land & sea

there are two words,

is this your note?

on one boat, "Amitié"

on the box, "Vincent"

In A Word

the unwriting:

she is losing her hold

the weight of her life too great

lightening her load, letting go of

her story, all that trying,

all that striving sliding away from her now

she is sliding away from her now

lighter lighter unwriting herself

losing her lines, wiping the slate

our conversations drift in one ear

                                       & out the other

their repetitions seem to soothe her

it's the sounds not the words

happy as i've ever known her

humming herself to her weightless death

motive:

all stories mis/stories, no story

without a motive, this is

what makes the killer interesting

      (emotion/commotion)

do we secretly identify

or virtuously disassociate?

either way it's relief we seek

      (motive, to push away; moment)

and what of authors' motives

beneath the motif —

hidden as ours?

      (these remain unnamed)

what we want

is a point of view

                    above the battle

far from stories we co-inhabit

with their

scratch and tear of

conflicting versions

*

then there's the man who

went to the store one fine sunday afternoon

for a carton of milk (for the wife)

or a pack of smokes (for the husband)

and never returned

vanished

no trace, no warning —

walked right out of his life —

abandoned his story mid-sentence.

a forerunner of reader response theory:

                                   up to you to invent the rest ...

gave the wife

the last word

(a gentlemanly gesture)

                        but
when she

had it, she

didn't want it —

        preferred

life as a sentence.

                        *

left to her own devices

all probable endings erased her

                                yet

she was the one

still in the story

*

the kids developed an annoying habit of

speaking in incomplete

sentences, as if she could

read their minds, as if one

day his voice would

reply from his

chair in the livingroom with

the correct dependent clause

*

see how seductive story is?

here i've begun telling one in the midst of

trying to loosen its grip

(writers escape artists)

and whether story entertains,

claims, blames or explains,

its instinct the same:

to keep sadness at bay.

details:

there are only so many stories

so many variations on a theme

is this why we cling to

story so stubbornly?

only details distinguish us

often details extinguish us

"now, words and ideas will always slip themselves

between me and the feeling,"

      us and

          others,

distinctions smoldering/searing like wildfire our

                                stories

                                     running ahead

we

    their smokey shadows

*

past tense = present tense = future tense =

a

tense situation.

narrative:

the long and the short of it

                                   longing is story

                                 story, longing.

if we relinquished story

would we be released?

is there a tabula rasa?

the narrative of our basic needs would remain;

its language of muscle,

nerve, sound

                            *

          "grammar ... mediates between sound and sense"

the question —

are we syntactically compatible?

the assumption —

if we're sound,

we make sense.

predicate —

"The part of the sentence or clause that expresses something about the subject: The house [is white]. The man [hit the dog]."

predicament —

the dog is tired of it.

semantic shift —

The dog [is white]. The house [hit the man].

*

the tower?

consciousness constructed with mental blocks.

*

to cross the continental divide

(where rivers flow in opposite directions)

come down off the continental shelf

see the artifacts of ancient cultures

the arbitrariness of what survives

their fragmented story lines

pieced
together

with the continental code of

archeologists', anthropologists', historians', and tourism's

poetic license

        (fault lines barely concealed)

get the

continental drift of

narrative nepotism

        *

there are

The Great Stories which endure,

and there are

the great stories which didn't concur and had

a short shelf life

*

to be captivated by story.

caught off guard by our dark horse longings;

carried away from our fenced-in plots.

to daydream the characters

of our other names —

langevity:

ourstories slip

through our fingers

leak away

yet

story

outlives us all

Shades of Meaning

1

light waves

        hellogood   hellogood   hellogood

            bye   bye   bye...

2

light is uncertain

its fingers reach through long shadows of lodgepole pines

the hush of high needles

is of no consolation

                                        who turned away first?

this is not a question of science

or season

3

fallen snow memory of light

4

flat light frightening

no depth of field

a word can mean anything, shed no light

fall

       with the thundering silence of snow

5

longlight lacks equanimity

                            illuminating one tree

leaving the next in the dark

                            splotching light on random trunks

with an abstractionist's

momentary abandon

                  circulating only in tree tops

far from the cold

unspeakable ground

6

this morning

halfway overhead

       sun becomes spotlight

       luminous trees lean into its promise

cast their shadows innocently

       (there is only so much light)

in surrounding chill

the others shudder

stutter — is it a question of

selection or position —

       the lightheaded trees

       murmur unreflectively:

       "your time will come"

7

to be fair

luminous trees can only drop

a limb in a storm

                    or sway

shadowed trees can twist

grow stunted,

or if not too old

                be uprooted, transplanted

                                in a different light

8

there

    is

this dark which holds all

          is

        this diffuse light

which absentmindedly sustains

          yet

        it's the warm-weightless embrace

            we dream of

9

mountains swallow sun fire-eater fast

their luminance suddenly a cold curtain

who are mountains?

failed light

absence of light

history of light hardbound?

who reveals more; conceals more?

who more than mountains

intimately knows

                          shades of meaning

10

before longlight

      a transitory tracing on wisps of lucent grass

before skins hardened

      a tender

      troubling ache

      of the familiar, then

we found ourselves

              light years apart

11

at twilight trees huddle together

tops swaying and singing their sutras

(keep us safe keep us safe keep us safe)

roots holding hands underground

at twilight there is forgiveness

for we are so much the same

12

this is more

than shadow & light

all these months i've avoided words for this

black & white on the page

for what drew us together drove us apart

there is no

          "in the light of day"

no

      "naked light"

only climatical predilections

and these fears to befriend

13

a quietening —

        low clouds

light the new snow

(all that falling beneath my feet)

        vision vertical

        recedes to

snow-stark fallen trees open casket still:

                death of forever

yet something grows in its place

what we name it

what we see

what we don't

        language a desperate thing

14

sullen sky today resolutely overcast;

"long, overlapping stitches to prevent ravelling"

15

to crawl between quilts of cloud & snow

                  shadow & light

eat the sweet pear of the tree thrice gone

for tree is generous & gives itself endlessly

seeds & recedes

even its ashes remember

concentric circled

alphabet

16

black & white

the wrong guy the right

even we disagree what this story is about and

i still trust silence more

17

in the

"infinite inner space of story ... is its soul"

Afterlife of the Heart

1

is every love story

a death story?

love sickness

on a death bed?

i want to say no —

not in the beginning

when there is no other left for

another — though with the first

       lovers' knot

we begin the slow disentangling

from our family affair, its

brooding ties

2

safety of the pack

becomes the chase:

          "I saw him looking at you"

"Oh, he's a deadhead"

(she's already in flight,

thinks of nothing else)

if she's lucky

there will be two —

          thrill of a dead heat

          and with the falling in

friendship's falling out

3

the multiplication table now

deadlocked by divisions of two

                romance

not this, not this —

all those years of imagining, reading, rehearsing;

all those movies all those songs

                there's no

going back

track, rewind, only

          dead ahead

4

have i convinced you

succeeded with my rationalization, ratio,

of romance's inexorable death rate?

like you, i never meant harm

yet the years go by:

the death count increases.

my comfort — the heart.

the heart alone

assures of an afterlife

reincarnates, reinvents itself beyond

each dead end

5

few things frighten us more than

love's death throes

does this explain

our virulent innocence?

though privately we admit failings

(o the humbling of years)

we leave

one another holding the

bag

the dead weight of

"if only"

6

let's face it

we have not only worn the death mask —

we've presented it

and though we abhor its perfect fit a

secret sweetness

is concealed

for behind our suffering

may be absolution

for the times

we walked away

our lips alight

7

two love birds mean

a bird in the house

killing two birds with one stone

merely a figure of speech

the two-chambered heart

wings its deafening beat

warnings unheeded

perceptions unfounded

care unnoticed in the

dead silence of betrayal

8

this is not lyrical

this is anything but lyrical

though sometimes

                much later

there's a

tender note

sounded,

        a recognition of one another

as long-lost friends

9

i write this now

for as Olson writes;

                                            "we stand more and more revealed"

this possibly

the greatest love we ever share

i write this now not

for all the love i have given but

for all the love given me

thought-lessly

i write this now

for the lover who holds me from behind

looks sky-eyed within

                              knowing

                                        on what ground we stand

The Sparkling Unsaid

the sparkling unsaid

the crystalline language of frost

waits on my morning window

fax transmitted in the night

conversation x-ray of

inside & outside pane

                                    it moved

up your windows as we talked

elegant yet indecipherable

                                        clung white

to dark hairs browing your mouth

as we walked your land

                                        your breathing

between our words

                        the sparkling unsaid

did you notice

how our gloved hands

fell into each other

                  then away

into

          then away

                        words

falling on deaf ears

heads hooded against

this biting clarity

                            etching & erasing

at its own will

in the snow

our tracks

still

this window

this window is where i think on you

solid pane below, six above

is it

the slope of the roof next door,

its snow-covered grace,

or the way

the elm limbs rise and twine

black & eager & longing?

this window

held the total eclipse

the night we spoke our desire,

three circles of

life briefly in line, darkness

moving deep inside

my mouth has imagined your mouth for so long

this window is where i think on you

where i look when you call,

eyes only

closing when over the line

in held silence

your body pulses into mine

could

the sound of skis through snow, fine-grained humming

movement in blue-slanted light

i follow your body in the distance

watch how you give yourself to these contours, how you

slide into this stunning sunset, its surprise

arousal red as cheeks cold and beneath layers of clothes

skins sweet with sweat while nearby

running fast river says could river sings could river sighs

could

snow-blowing-snow

snow blows across the Rosetown highway

                                        the road goes somewhere

the snow, nowhere

it blows diagonally toward my car, fluid and mesmerizing

i feel the pull of

this white seduction lightly ever so lightly around my body

as the road's black purposefulness disappears,

concentrate on signs, other determined cars

                                        the real goes somewhere

yet snow-blowing-snow

is where i want to go

boundary

the black cross signals me to

turn, push into fluid blue

            breath/stroke

my body the boundary between two mediums

       water's wet kiss/your mouth

               yet lungs lust air

wall, black cross reminds

turn, push into

       breath/stroke

ripples' reflections dancing bottom of pool

he loved to watch,

his body stroke-stiffened in Arizona lawnchair

his eyes

      your's

           winter afternoon Ascension blue

black

(the presence of all colour)

cross

wall

("yes; no —") tropos,

turn, push into

breath/stroke

my body the boundary/"hold me in my uncertainty"

i think cross

breath/stroke

how you touch me

this blue all around

the clouds will bring you

the clouds will bring you

how i love the breeze the breadth the breath of you

the clouds will sing you

the shape the shift the soak of you

in te non deficit ullum gaudium

in you there is no shortage of joy

in your mouth

dew the rain the flood of you

in your body

i am immersed in warm moisture of you

the clouds will bring you

gathering, dispersing breezes of pleasure into your womb

articulated air will sing you

your resonate words caressing my boughs

all language is longing

here is here

                    there is there

this one breath

                    tells me so

then the next —

here is here

                    there is there

with each hello

                    a goodbye

to before, between, last time

                              the blackeyed susans

held the road

(your name, gaze)

               white butterflies rushed to us speeding by

their bodies a torn letter

on the altar of your car

we hold images close

as if they were one another's bodies

yet sleep alone

neither here

nor there

this poem in defiance of

exhale &

inhale

all language is longing

Cloudnotes

altocumulus

i prepare my heart for you

am learning to read the clouds for instruction

                              altocumulus considers moisture

              considers sun

from the palm of a dune

i watch them form, darken, shift

this morning i awoke repeating your number

rhythmic as waves

a voice also comes:

                    "expect nothing"

                    "forget everything"

altocumulus considers moisture considers sun

in the dunes at Outlook

lying in sun's first warmth

you soon to leave

the gulls the

Saskatchewan lapping

cirrus sighed content overhead

as i held you long in nothing said

mixed skies

"I was hoping you'd call"

we talk

with shore's need for sea's endless caress

longing

rising receding rising

as the plates beneath

grind and shift

sadness relief aftershock joy

mixed skies this morning

altocumulus

a bit of blue down wind

stratocumulus undulatus

(grey water-droplet clouds)

your long silence after

i prepare my heart for you

tears cresting through days of sea and ferries,

roads. mountains, and prairies

"... I prepare my heart for you"

mixed skies again

on a silver band

raven and eagle are beak to beak

    sky surrounds them

altocumulus, stratocumulus,

cumulonimbus with virga

        and praecipitatio reaching the ground

    our first night

     "I just want to lie beside you"

tentativeness so daring, touching

        your breathing

    staccato

until you settled nose to nose

        inhaling

exhaling

our sleep-soft breath

                                                tideline

the sea exhales two conch, an agate,

stone of starry night, stone of

sand with fossils shining black and

small triangular blood stone

                                        (piece of my heart)

                    for you for

                                you

cirrus thoughts

i thought of you

        and came

i thought of you and

        came again

the thought of you

       came to me

          your tongue

            a wild strawberry

nimbostratus

jagged slateblue nimbostratus opacus

        press down

                relinquish rain

forest revels green

beneath its

sheltering canopy

raven calls

        i answer

      calls

          i answer

   call

     answer

at the mouth of the tea-brown Tlell

the silver kiss of Hecate Strait

              immature eagle feather

floats to me

nimbostratus again

dew point

nimbostratus praecipitatio inhales trees, sea

lifts opalescent exhaling layers and layers of

clouds, mountains into Skidegate Inlet

nimbostratus praecipitatio inhales again

distance forgotten in the soft embrace of near

yet you circle within

dove after the flood

sea level

Queen Charlotte Sandspit Lanscoone Rennel Beresford Langara

six fault lines murmuring below

i tell you

you say "like my life feels"

and

      "be careful"

as if

i say

"that's why it's so powerful here"

                        Ring of Fire

          (geologies' integrity)

portholes of cirrus

early out on its polished curvilinearity

        surface and reflective colour

in perfect sensuous harmony

(Brancusi would weep)

                this close —

it is not flat but undulating

all lived and living lungs contracting,

expanding in hypnotic syncopation

            this close —

the morning i awoke

everything moving

trembling for weeks

       months later

           i recognized you

               curve and motion

nimbostratus surrenders to altocumulus to

portholes of cirrus and

stratocumulus bluesky eyes

there and

there

and there

watching

like eagles sentinel in shoreline spruce

in the abandoned village of Skedans (Raven Village)

Haida Watchman Charlie Wesley tells of

disease, missionaries burning poles

taking children

this close —

to destruction

his quiet humour

a porthole or eye

in a long-grey stormy sky

sky dark

waves wake me

      rock me with increasing intensity

this close —

        there is only the being in it

nothing to be done, my body's violent

      trembling calms recognizing motion sickness for fear

there are those i have harmed

              i wing dream messages to them

there are those who have looked long into the face of fear

        i thank them

there is you

      this close —

        heart is not beat

        but tremor

What Holds Us Here

even mountains tremble

i wanted to write about mountains

                              intended to

write about one particular mountain

its shifting sensuality

seductive solidness beneath

                        i'm leaning

into the illusion of your irrefutable presence immovable

as a mountain

                  yet this mountain has cleft

crevice labial

spinal slide vertiginous vertebrae a vertex to vortex inclination that

magnetizes me and i've heard when

lightning factures sky

even mountains tremble

iambic heart

you are not here and,

once again, i am not there, and

there is all this space between though

Raimundo says "Spatiality ... makes nearness possible"

                                              at this moment

i sit in the space (literal) in which you sat (literal)

nearly a year ago when

you received my note

with those eight letters the heart hungers for

                  (the heart insatiate)

though they frightened you

                    when hunger strikes

                   we fall into step with

iambic heart's

               love me/love me/love me

muse mute

see all these words? see how foolishly i try to transmute

your muteness? absence not alchemical unless you imagine

incantation rivals incarnation. i myself do not, have no

illusion, no aspiration to reinvent you with word and

breath.

lost in the translation

secondary sources

rarely ressemble

the raw material

zero gravity

there is this spaciousness about you, in you, with you,

which words litter like space satellite and shuttle debris

each letter forever floating aimlessly

breathing spell

breathing space

our first gentleness

the in

& out of

one another's galaxies

"who could live if space were not bliss?"

quartet of lungs

crest & trough their breathing spell

memory of tears

after all that struggle not a pat on the back

but a slap

is this why babies cry,

or does catching one's breath hurt?

no time for amphibious ambivalence

                                ("living a double life")

first it's fluid then air and a

separateness only tears speak

what holds us here

holding your breath is useless

we are this in-betweenness this

movement of inner & outer space this

inhale & exhale conversion this

inspire & expire motion this

is what sustains us

we can live without love without

food without water (for periods of time)

                                            but without air

we begin to self-destruct

within three minutes

oxygen

"essential for plant and animal respiration"

is   what holds us here

your name written on it

breath is said to be spirit

is this why you haunt me?

clouds are said to be spirits

is this why we're intrigued by

                seeing our breath?

that first winter walk

our spirits clung to the crystals before us

                "breath is the journey"

and when

you took my breath

away in the dark

i was not afraid

you gave it back

your name written on it as i

gave you yours

with mine

Dark Thoughts

in the bluegreen darkening

last night in the bluegreen darkening

i talked with a stranger

whose image slowly receded

into the silent thickening

filling in the blanks between lodgepole pines

without eyes' outline of assumption

body burrows into voice

                                voice

feeling its way like roots underground

with each reaching out

                        voice

must make decisions,

habits of body language

no assistance in the dark

camouflage of veins & flesh, hair & cloth forgotten

voice becomes airborne-tactile

words — after all

only sound

      shape   motion feeling

we say things in the dark that

embarrass us by light of day, we

say things in that dark that

alter our lives irrevocably

voice resides in darkness

recognizes its element

the question being

in the light of day

do we recognize ourselves?

the shoulder of darkness

on the shoulder of darkness

                          white-eyes flash

stare momentarily mesmerized by

headlights' speeding glare

                          i grip

the wheel:

            "don't bolt!   don't swerve!"

                              everything suspended in

this second or two   this shock of

skins suddenly heading for one another   skins

which want nothing to do with one another   skins

startled by glimpsing the flimsy fiction of   their will, their

separateness, by this near collision of their

daydream-insular-selves

origin of contra/diction

the body the origin of contra/diction

its vital workings

kept in the dark

      while

its container

thrives on light

      an urgent discrepancy

negotiated by the

      in-between of our orifices

      (public & private) around

      the clock

      foot in the door

      ("i was waiting for an opening")

our hollows

sites of our commerce

      (import/export)

"i want; you want"

these imperatives

cite our confusion

which is

our unbearable loneliness   each

as thin-skinned   as

the other

strange

our fear of the dark when

this is where we live

the body the

dark continent

so familiar, so

unknowable, its

language

two skins

touching

weightlifting

lifting barbells muscles know their limits

only coaxing of

regular workouts increase their capacity

incrementally   over time

                    at the heart of the matter

                            the heart

the body envelops it: tissue   fluid   bone   its troposphere

                    nonluminous sphere the

                        heart of darkness

a muscular organ we fail

to recognize the limits of

(too much exertion;

too little patience), the

heavy heart

sheer muscular exhaustion

the heart has a circulatory orbit

(cautious as any muscle)

         memory its meaning

midway across lake-umbra

midway across lake-umbra you ask

"how deep is it here?"

                Lise replying "I'll tell you

                when we've reached the shore"

    me interjecting between strokes

    "it only takes a few inches ...

    after that, it doesn't matter"

            Lac du Cafe

            only a few ripples

            beyond a pond

its water fragrant   velvet a

            solitary sigh

that night

on the lip of the lake

we watch sky unloosen the reassuring

"each star in its appointed place"

cross it out

with every gasp-provoking meteor

hurtling-brilliant and unpredictable through blackazure

atmosphere

underscoring again, again & again ...

it only takes a few moments

something

luxurious-simple

soft beating within   then Lise

begins singing Minnesota camp songs

made-up by twelve-year-old girls on their "Canadian"

(Lise staying behind on her bunkbed, reading

The Aeneid, while they paddled & sang their hearts out in

to the shimmering unknown)   Lise

some-thirty years later   still

carries their songs —

adolescent thrill astonishingly intact —

                              "We've seen everything from lakes to stars

                              But the gems we treasure most by far,

                              Are the friendships that became so dear:

                              Jewels of Canada."

two weeks later i phone from the mountains

"you never did say how deep Lac du Cafe is"

her laughter told me before her words

"a hundred and thirty feet"

how bodies leave ecstatic marks

how bodies leave ecstatic marks more on one

another in the dark

how vision depends on total eclipse of

our twin planet eyes

how fear of the dark not of the unknown   but of our

imagination's disquieting reality

dawn & dusk our respite

dawn & dusk our respite

in daylight

we colour determinedly inside the lines:

> This is woman.
>
> This is tree.
>
> This is animal.

in darkness

we anxiously finger our way unnerved we

may

> share the same skin

Yellow the Sweet Ache

yellow the sweet ache

through the season of greening wildflowers

bloom in waves of different colours

in your absence yellow has opened everywhere though

wildroses still fling their perfect hues ... yellow the

sweet ache i feel for you

sweet-sue-so-sweet

that song i had wondered about for weeks suddenly

perched in front of me before you left

yellow warbler yellow warbler is this what yellow sounds like:

"High pitched, pattern song of three similar notes followed by

sweet-sweet-sweet-sue-so-sweet"

bzzz...

refrigerator's humm furnace's lowrumble the clay coloured sparrow's "bzzz"

this season's sustained bass note (its song "insectlike")

is this foraging-voice-camouflage or

emulation, ovation for those it relishes?

when i think of your mouth i know the answer

wildrose buds

expectant pink of wildrose buds taunt me most their sepals'

sensuous-green-adagio to warmth, slow-motion-desire exquisite

anticipation of the in-between

how your lips swell and part beneath the heat of my breath

shameless they are utterly shameless, i look the other way

no caboose in sight

picking up speed trains pass along the edge of your land as

i'm thinking how you are one-long-lesson-in-longing no caboose in sight

i'm waiting for that moan rising from accelerating

rumble — that way back in from the beginning of time crescendoing

— i'm waiting for you to come home. come; home.

Publishing Credits

"Shades of Meaning" will appear in *Poetry Canada*, volume 16, # 2, 1998.

"Afterlife of the Heart" appeared in *Rampike*, volume 8/#2, 1997.

"What Holds Us Here" (four poems) appeared in *The Malahat Review*, # 114, Spring 1996.

"The Sparkling Unsaid" appeared in *Arc*, # 36, Spring 1996.

"Cloudnotes" appeared in *The Capilano Review*, Series 2, # 16, Summer 1995.

"Yellow the Sweet Ache" appeared in *Fireweed*, Issue 56, Late Winter 1996.

Credits for quotes

"In A Word" ("details:"), J. Winterson, *The Passion*; Henry Carr Pearson, Mary Frederika Kirchwey *Essentials of English*

"Shades of Meaning" (poem 16), T. Moore, *Care of The Soul*.

"The Sparkling Unsaid" ("the clouds will bring you"), Latin words by Hildegard Von Bingen.

"What Holds Us Here": ("iambic heart"), R. Pannikar, "There Is No Outer without Inner Space," *Cross Currents*, Spring 1993; ("breathing spell"), *Taiftiriya Upsanishad*, II, 7,2; ("your name written on it"), Endre Farkas, from poem written on the wall of Cardinal Studio, The Banff Centre.

142

For their support for and comments on this manuscript I would like to thank Di Brandt, Sylvia Legris, Mary Meigs, Susan Shantz, Cheryl Sourkes, Steven Warland and Lise Weil.

About the cover

Cover: Detail from Dorrit Jacoby: *Flying Woman* (1992). Mixed media, 40 x 50 cm. Private collection. From a photgraph by Judy Bowyer.

Dorrit Jacoby is an Israeli-Canadian artist and mother of four who has worked in Arad for the past 20 years. Her work has been exhibited in important museums and gallaries in Germany, the United States, Canada, Japan, Taiwan, Singapore, Thailand, Korea and Isreal. She has received numerous scholarships and awards, both in Canada and Israel. Jacoby works outdoors, in the desert, exposed to nature's forces and the elements. Her personal experience serves as an integral part of her typically multi-layered, highly feminine works which are characterized by a strong sense of totality.

About *Flying Woman*:

An ancient tale recounts the story of a woman who swallowed children and was condemned to die. Her stomach was cut open and filled with knives, but she kept on flying. Her mouth was filled with stones, a stake was driven through her cheek and she was forced to the ground, but no one could kill her soul, and she kept on flying.